中国天然气发展报告

（2020）

国家能源局石油天然气司

国务院发展研究中心资源与环境政策研究所

自然资源部油气资源战略研究中心

石油工业出版社

图书在版编目（CIP）数据

中国天然气发展报告.2020/国家能源局石油天然气司，国务院发展研究中心资源与环境政策研究所，自然资源部油气资源战略研究中心编.—北京：石油工业出版社，2020.9

ISBN 978-7-5183-4183-2

Ⅰ.①中⋯ Ⅱ.①国⋯②国⋯③自⋯ Ⅲ.①天然气工业—研究报告—中国—2020 Ⅳ.①F426.22

中国版本图书馆CIP数据核字（2020）第162789号

出版发行：石油工业出版社
　　　　　（北京市朝阳区安华里二区1号楼 100011）
网　　址：http://www.petropub.com
编　辑　部：(010) 64523546　图书营销中心：(010) 64523633
经　　销：全国新华书店
印　　刷：北京中石油彩色印刷有限责任公司

2020年9月第1版　2020年9月第1次印刷
787×1092毫米　开本：1/16　印张：4.25
字数：88千字

定　价：50.00元
（如发现印装质量问题，我社图书营销中心负责调换）
版权所有，翻印必究

《中国天然气发展报告（2020）》编委会

（以下按姓氏笔画排序）

主　任：
　　刘宝华　凌月明　隆国强

副主任：
　　刘　红　高世楫　谢承祥

委　员：
　　王　晶　叶国标　李　铮　李英华
　　李继峰　张应红　武文来　郑和荣
　　周　鹏　郭焦锋　韩景宽　潘继平

总协调人：
　　郭焦锋

编写单位：
　　国家能源局石油天然气司
　　国务院发展研究中心资源与环境政策研究所
　　自然资源部油气资源战略研究中心

支持单位：
　　中国石油大学（华东）
　　住房和城乡建设部标准定额研究所
　　中国石油规划总院
　　中国石化石油勘探开发研究院
　　中海石油气电集团有限责任公司
　　上海石油天然气交易中心

出版和翻译单位：
　　石油工业出版社

前　言

当前世界天然气供需格局正面临深度调整。天然气资源供应进一步宽松，市场竞争加剧，国际贸易方式更加灵活，价格持续下降。2020年初以来，新型冠状病毒肺炎疫情（以下简称"新冠疫情"）蔓延，世界经济衰退，国际天然气贸易量萎缩，价格大幅波动。保障供应安全、稳定市场消费成为当前世界天然气发展的新焦点。

2019年是中华人民共和国成立70周年，也是"四个革命、一个合作"能源安全新战略实施5周年。各部门、各地方和企业认真贯彻落实党中央、国务院决策部署，大力提升油气勘探开发力度和加快天然气产供储销体系建设都取得明显成效。2019年是"十三五"勘探开发投资最大的一年，也是天然气储产量增长成绩最好的一年。国家油气管网公司组建成立，标志着"管住中间、放开两头"的油气体制改革迈出关键一步。面对新冠疫情的冲击，各方主动作为，全力保障天然气稳定供应，为疫情防控和经济社会稳定发展提供有力支撑。

下一步，围绕"六稳""六保"工作大局，聚焦天然气产供储销体系建设，将继续大力提升勘探开发力度，加快完善管网配套改革，补齐储气能力短板，推动天然气高质量发展。

目 录

一、2019 年国内外天然气产业稳定发展 ·················· 1

（一）世界天然气发展状况 ························· 1

（二）中国天然气发展状况 ························· 3

二、2019 年中国天然气市场化改革进程加快 ················ 6

（一）天然气上游市场化改革 ······················· 6

（二）天然气中游市场化改革 ······················· 7

（三）天然气下游市场化改革 ······················· 8

三、2020 年中国天然气产业逆势前行 ···················· 12

（一）2020 年上半年发展回顾 ······················ 12

（二）2020 年下半年中国天然气发展形势展望 ············· 13

结束语 ·· 16

一、2019年国内外天然气产业稳定发展[1]

2019年，世界天然气继续保持供需宽松态势，贸易量较快增长，长协合同条款更加灵活，定价方式更趋多元，LNG现货占比进一步提升。中国天然气产供储销体系继续完善，加大勘探开发力度成效显著，管道、储气等重大基础设施加快推进，消费规模持续攀升，冬季高峰期用气得到有效保障。

（一）世界天然气发展状况

产量稳步增加，液化能力快速提升。 世界天然气勘探取得了多个重大发现，海域仍为天然气发现热点领域。2019年，世界新增天然气可采储量2.1万亿立方米，约71.0%分布在海域。截至2019年底，世界天然气剩余可采储量为198.8万亿立方米，储采比为49.8，天然气产量为3.99万亿立方米，同比增长3.4%，增速下降1.6个百分点。其中，北美地区天然气产量为11280亿立方米，同比增长7.4%；中东地区天然气产量为6953亿立方米，同比增长2.1%；俄罗斯—中亚地区天然气产量为8465亿立方米，同比增长1.9%。世界天然气液化能力达4.33亿吨/年，同比增长9.5%，增速上升1.7个百分点。新增10个LNG出口终端项目，共有11条生产线

---

[1] 本节世界天然气储量、生产、消费和贸易的数量及增速主要来源于《BP世界能源统计（2020）》，天然气液化能力和项目的数据来自埃信华迈（IHS）；LNG贸易合同定价与油价挂钩的数据来自FGE公司；中国天然气储量数据来源于自然资源部《全国油气矿产储量通报（2019）》。中国天然气产量数据来源于国家发展和改革委员会（简称国家发展改革委）和国家统计局，天然气进出口数据来源于国家海关总署。

投产，新增产能 3781 万吨 / 年，同比增长 21.4%，主要集中在美国、俄罗斯和澳大利亚，其中 59.8% 的新增产能在美国。

消费增速回落，北美和亚太地区增速放缓。 2019 年，世界天然气消费量为 3.93 万亿立方米，同比增长 2.0%，增速下降 3.3 个百分点，在一次能源消费中占比为 24.2%。北美地区天然气消费量为 10576 亿立方米，同比增长 3.1%，其中美国天然气消费量为 8466 亿立方米，同比增长 3.3%，增速下降 7.5 个百分点，主要原因是冬季气温相对较高，采暖用气需求增长放缓；亚太地区天然气消费量为 8699 亿立方米，同比增长 4.7%，其中日本天然气消费量为 1081 亿立方米，同比下降 6.6%，主要原因是日本重启核电站，减少天然气消费；欧洲天然气消费量为 5541 亿立方米，同比增长 1.1%，主要原因是欧洲碳价上涨近 70%，加之气价走低，天然气发电经济性显现，有力拉动了天然气需求。

贸易量持续增长，LNG 贸易量增长较快。 2019 年，世界天然气贸易量为 1.29 万亿立方米，同比增长 4.1%，贸易量占世界天然气消费量的 32.7%，同比提高 0.6 个百分点。其中，管道气贸易量为 8015 亿立方米，同比下降 0.5%；LNG 贸易量为 4851 亿立方米，同比增长 12.7%。2019 年，世界 LNG 现货贸易量占 LNG 贸易总量的 33.5%。LNG 出口量排名前五的国家分别为卡塔尔（1071 亿立方米）、澳大利亚（1047 亿立方米）、美国（475 亿立方米）、俄罗斯（394 亿立方米）和马来西亚（351 亿立方米）。2019 年，LNG 出口总增量为

545亿立方米，其中美国、俄罗斯和澳大利亚LNG出口增量位列前三，分别增加189亿立方米、144亿立方米和129亿立方米。LNG进口量排名前三的国家分别为日本（1055亿立方米）、中国（848亿立方米）和韩国（556亿立方米）；LNG进口增量排名前三的国家分别为中国（113亿立方米）、英国（109亿立方米）和法国（101亿立方米）。

价格低位运行，合同形式更加灵活。 2019年，天然气供需较为宽松，价格低位运行。美国亨利中心天然气年均价格为2.53美元/百万英热单位，同比下跌19.0%。英国NBP年均价格为4.45美元/百万英热单位，同比下跌44.3%。东北亚地区长协年均价格为9.43美元/百万英热单位，同比下跌1.0%；LNG现货年均价格为5.95美元/百万英热单位，同比下跌39.1%。2019年执行的合同中，供应商以资源池模式供应的合同量占比达18.5%；世界新签合同中不限制目的地的合同量占比近90.0%。

（二）中国天然气发展状况

中国天然气勘探开发力度明显加大，储量和产量增幅均创历史纪录。 2019年，全国油气勘探开发投资达3348亿元，同比增长25.5%，其中勘探投资达821亿元，创历史新高。常规天然气勘探取得一系列重大成果，相继在四川盆地、鄂尔多斯盆地、塔里木盆地及海域等获得重要发现，有望新增一批规模储量资源区；页岩气在四川盆地长宁—威远、太阳等区块获得突破，南川地区实现了常压页岩气勘探新发现。

全国新增天然气探明地质储量 1.58 万亿立方米，同比增加约 6000 亿立方米，创历史纪录。其中，常规天然气新增探明地质储量 8091 亿立方米，新增技术可采储量 3521 亿立方米；页岩气新增探明地质储量 7644 亿立方米，新增技术可采储量 1838 亿立方米。全国天然气（含非常规气）产量达 1773 亿立方米，同比增加 170 亿立方米，创历史新高，其中常规气产量为 1527 亿立方米，页岩气产量为 154 亿立方米，煤层气产量为 55 亿立方米，煤制气产量为 36.8 亿立方米。

进口稳步增长，进口来源和主体日趋多元。2019 年，中国进口天然气 9656 万吨❶（折合 1352 亿立方米），同比增加 6.9%。从进口构成看，管道气进口 3631 万吨（折合 508 亿立方米❷），占比为 37.6%；LNG 进口 6025 万吨，占比为 62.4%。LNG 进口来源更加多元，澳大利亚是最大的进口来源国（2910 万吨），其次是卡塔尔（863 万吨）和马来西亚（737 万吨）；LNG 现货比例进一步提升，LNG 现货进口量为 2130 万吨，占 LNG 总进口量的 35.4%。天然气进口市场主体有所增加，除主要油气企业外，地方国有、民营和港资企业等共进口 LNG 441 万吨，占全国 LNG 进口总量的 7.3%。

基础设施布局进一步完善，互联互通继续推进。截至 2019 年底，中国建成干线输气管道超过 8.7 万千米，一次输气能力超过 3500 亿立方米/年。中俄东线北段工程建成投产，

---

❶ 全国年度进口总量及价格数据均来自海关总署；分国家及企业进口数据来源于 IHS 统计数据库。
❷ 折算系数为：1 吨=1400 立方米。

标志着东北、西北、西南、海上四大进口通道都同时具备了油气进口能力。北方重点地区多渠道、多气源供应格局继续完善，应急供气能力进一步提升，西气东输二线广州站反输增压完成改造；陕京四线三座压气站投产；鄂安沧管道一期投产。截至2019年底，全国建成地下储气库27座，有效工作气量达102亿立方米，同比增长超过30亿立方米。

消费规模持续扩大，增速有所放缓。 2019年，天然气表观消费量为3064亿立方米，同比增长8.6%，在一次能源消费结构中占比达8.1%，同比上升0.3个百分点。从消费结构看，城市燃气和工业用气仍是天然气消费的主力，分别占全国消费量的37.2%和35.0%；化工用气增速有所回升，发电用气增速阶段性回落。从消费区域看，华东地区是全国消费量最大的区域，全年消费量达897亿立方米，占全国消费量的29.2%；其次是华北、西北和西南地区，消费量分别为598亿立方米、396亿立方米和375亿立方米。从省消费量看，13个省份用气量超过100亿立方米，其中江苏超过300亿立方米，广东、四川都超过200亿立方米。

二、2019年中国天然气市场化改革进程加快

2019年以来，中国持续推进天然气市场化改革。上游环节放宽市场准入，全面推进矿业权竞争性出让，激发勘探开发活力。中游环节实施运销分离，组建国家油气管网公司，进一步推进基础设施向第三方公平开放。下游环节深化天然气价格改革，实施减税降费，扩大天然气利用。

（一）天然气上游市场化改革

深化油气上游市场化改革，有序放开油气勘探开发市场。 贯彻落实党中央、国务院关于深化油气体制改革、大力提升油气勘探开发力度精神，先后出台了《关于统筹推进自然资源资产产权制度改革的指导意见》《外商投资准入特别管理措施（负面清单）（2019年版）》《自然资源部关于推进矿产资源管理改革若干事项的意见（试行）》，开放油气勘查开采市场，多渠道引入社会资金开展油气勘探开发；实行更加严格的区块退出，督促企业加大勘探开发力度；实行油气探采合一制度，从制度层面保障企业勘探获得发现后直接进入油气开采；将探矿权2年延续1次调整为5年延续1次，减轻企业办事成本；将煤层气矿业权出让登记权限下放至省级自然资源主管部门，调动地方积极性。从2019年7月30日起，外资进入中国油气勘探开发等领域的限制进一步放宽，油气勘探开发限于合资、合作的限制逐步取消。继续推进新

疆试点，持续推进黔北页岩气试验区、川南页岩气试验区建设，设立鄂西页岩气勘探开发综合示范区，推进南海油气勘查开采改革试点及山西开展能源革命综合改革试点工作。

完善非常规天然气补贴政策，鼓励企业加快非常规气开发。《关于〈可再生能源发展专项资金管理暂行办法〉的补充通知》明确，设置可再生能源发展专项资金支持煤层气（煤矿瓦斯）、页岩气、致密气等非常规天然气开采利用，对超过上年产量的，按超额程度给予梯级奖补；对未达到上年产量的，按程度扣减；对取暖季生产的非常规天然气增量部分，给予超额系数折算，体现"冬增冬补"。

（二）天然气中游市场化改革

组建国家油气管网公司，推进"全国一张网"建设。认真落实《关于深化石油天然气体制改革的若干意见》《石油天然气管网运营机制改革实施意见》等文件精神，组建国有资本控股、投资主体多元化的石油天然气管网公司。深化体制机制改革，出台《油气管网设施公平开放监管办法》，加快实现基础设施互联互通和公平开放，建设油气管网设施公平开放信息平台，确保信息获取公开透明，优化市场运行环境。随着国家油气管网公司的设立和其他各级各类长输管道运销分离，有利于实现管网等中游基础设施向第三方市场主体的公平开放；有利于进一步加快统筹全国油气干线管网规划建设运营，促进管网互联互通，构建"全国一张网"；有利于进一步提高油气资源运输和配置效率，保障油气安全稳定供应。

出台《关于加快推进天然气储备能力建设的实施意见》等文件，进一步加快推进储气基础设施建设，提升天然气储备能力。优化储气设施规划建设布局，引导峰谷差大、需求增长快的地区适当提高建设目标。建立健全储气设施运营模式，推行独立运营，完善价格机制等投资回收渠道。加大土地、财税、金融、投资等政策支持力度，激励企业加速补足储气基础设施建设短板，促进储气能力快速提升。

（三）天然气下游市场化改革

因地制宜推进天然气发电和加快发展交通用气，持续发挥天然气对大气污染防治的积极作用。兼顾不同地区、不同资源禀赋条件、不同用能方式的协调发展，稳步推进天然气发电项目建设。截至 2019 年底，天然气发电装机已超过 9000 万千瓦。同时《2020 年全球船用燃油限硫令实施方案》等文件加速了船舶低硫燃料的推广应用，随着"中国版限硫令"于 2020 年 1 月 1 日生效实施，LNG 船舶和 LNG 重型卡车有望持续发展。

有效实施减税降费，终端用户切实享受改革红利。《关于调整天然气基准门站价格的通知》等文件要求，根据增值税率调整情况（天然气税率降至 9%），充分考虑增值税率降低因素对应调整各省（区、市）天然气基准门站价格，确保将增值税率调低部分的红利归于用户。规定城镇燃气工程安装收费标准，原则上成本利润率不得超过 10%，以此降低天然气终端用户用气成本，引导城镇燃气企业转型升级和高质量发展。2020年2月印发通知，在现行天然气价格机制框架内，提前实行淡季价格政策，阶段性降低企业用气成本。

专栏

天然气上游市场化改革政策

序号	发布时间	发布单位	政策名称
1	2019年1月	科技部、财政部	《关于进一步优化国家重点研发计划项目和资金管理的通知》（国科发资〔2019〕45号）
2	2019年2月	国务院	《国务院关于取消和下放一批行政许可事项的决定》（国发〔2019〕6号）
3	2019年4月	中共中央办公厅、国务院办公厅	《关于统筹推进自然资源资产产权制度改革的指导意见》
4	2019年6月	国家发展改革委、商务部	《外商投资准入特别管理措施（负面清单）（2019年版）》（国家发展改革委、商务部令第25号）
5	2019年6月	国家发展改革委、商务部	《自由贸易试验区外商投资准入特别管理措施（负面清单）（2019年版）》（国家发展改革委、商务部令第26号）
6	2019年6月	国家发展改革委、商务部	《鼓励外商投资产业目录（2019年版）》（国家发展改革委、商务部令第27号）
7	2019年6月	财政部	《关于〈可再生能源发展专项资金管理暂行办法〉的补充通知》（财建〔2019〕298号）
8	2019年12月	自然资源部	《自然资源部关于推进矿产资源管理改革若干事项的意见（试行）》（自然资规〔2019〕7号）

续表

序号	发布时间	发布单位	政策名称
9	2019年12月	国家能源局	《能源领域首台（套）重大技术装备评定和评价办法（试行）》（国能发科技〔2019〕89号）
10	2020年3月	财政部、海关总署、税务总局	《关于取消海洋石油（天然气）开采项目免税进口额度管理的通知》（财关税〔2020〕5号）
11	2020年3月	财政部、海关总署、税务总局	《关于取消陆上特定地区石油（天然气）开采项目免税进口额度管理的通知》（财关税〔2020〕6号）

天然气中游市场化改革政策

序号	发布时间	发布单位	政策名称
1	2019年3月	中央全面深化改革委员会	《石油天然气管网运营机制改革实施意见》
2	2019年5月	国家发展改革委、国家能源局、住房和城乡建设部、市场监管总局	《油气管网设施公平开放监管办法》（发改能源规〔2019〕916号）
3	2019年10月	国家能源局	《关于加强天然气管网设施公平开放相关信息公开工作的通知》（国能综通监管〔2019〕76号）
4	2019年12月	国家发展改革委	《中央定价目录》（国家发展改革委令第29号）

续表

序号	发布时间	发布单位	政策名称
5	2020年4月	国家发展改革委、财政部、自然资源部、住房和城乡建设部、国家能源局	《关于加快推进天然气储备能力建设的实施意见》（发改价格〔2020〕567号）
6	2020年5月	中共中央、国务院	《关于新时代加快完善社会主义市场经济体制的意见》

天然气下游市场化改革政策

序号	发布时间	发布单位	政策名称
1	2019年3月	国家发展改革委	《关于调整天然气基准门站价格的通知》（发改价格〔2019〕562号）
2	2019年6月	国家发展改革委、住房和城乡建设部、市场监管总局	《关于规范城镇燃气工程安装收费的指导意见》（发改价格〔2019〕1131号）
3	2019年6月	国家发展改革委、商务部	《外商投资准入特别管理措施（负面清单）（2019年版）》（国家发展改革委、商务部令第25号）
4	2019年10月	国家海事局	《2020年全球船用燃油限硫令实施方案》（海事局公告第20号）
5	2020年2月	国家发展改革委	《关于阶段性降低非居民用气成本支持企业复工复产的通知》（发改价格〔2020〕257号）

三、2020 年中国天然气产业逆势前行

2020 年以来，新冠疫情暴发对中国经济社会和能源发展带来阶段性较大影响。天然气需求增速明显放缓，但上半年仍实现 1.5% 的正增长。2020 年是"十三五"收官之年，也是"十四五"谋划之年。天然气产业要按照"四个革命、一个合作"能源安全新战略重要部署，继续推进行业高质量发展。

（一）2020 年上半年发展回顾

能源保供在疫情中经受考验，上半年天然气消费实现同比正增长。 一季度，中国经济增长 –6.8%，第二、第三产业增加值分别下降 9.6% 和 5.2%；上半年经济增长 –1.6%，第二、第三产业增加值分别下降 1.9% 和 1.6%。2020 年上半年，受疫情和油价下行叠加影响，国内油气行业面临冲击和挑战。各部门、地方和企业全力配合，合力打赢油气领域抗疫保供攻坚战，坚决保障抗疫主战区和全国用油用气需求。天然气产供储销体系建设稳步推进，科学决策，扎实有序做好中俄东线等基础设施重大项目和互联互通工程复工复产，中俄东线中段等重大工程按既定节点有序推进。2020 年上半年，天然气消费仍保持正增长，同比增长 1.5% 左右。推动天然气消费正增长的因素包括：国内外气价走低，天然气价格竞争力凸显；城镇燃气受疫情冲击较小，且北方部分省市供暖季延长；二季度以来经济复苏态势明显，复工复产带动工业、发电等用气稳中有升。

2020年上半年，中国天然气勘探力度基本不变而产量继续强劲增长。面对新冠疫情带来的新挑战、新困难，2020年上半年全国油气勘探开发投资总体稳定，勘探工作量稳中有增，继续在四川、塔里木等盆地获得重要发现；天然气产量达940亿立方米，同比增长10.3%，其中常规气产量为823亿立方米，同比增长约8%，页岩气产量为91亿立方米，同比增长约35%，煤层气产量为26亿立方米，同比增长约10%。预计2020年中国天然气产量为1890亿立方米（不包括煤制气），同比增长约9%，总体保持较快增长态势。

2020年上半年，天然气需求结构化差异走势明显。一是工业用气从负增长逐步恢复至2019年同期水平。新冠疫情暴发初期，工业用气受到一定冲击，随后国家实施了阶段性降低非居民气价等政策，降低企业用气成本，工业用气逐月回升，1—6月累计用气量已恢复到2019年的同期水平。二是城镇燃气保持稳定增长。一季度受北方部分省市供暖季延长的拉动影响，城镇燃气保持稳定增长；二季度随各地先后下调防控级别，流动人口持续增加，商场、餐馆、学校等逐步恢复运行，公共服务部门的天然气需求显著提升，两者共同推动上半年城镇燃气同比增长超过10%。三是发电用气和化工用气受疫情影响相对明显，上半年有所下降。

（二）2020年下半年中国天然气发展形势展望

2020年下半年，面对新冠疫情冲击，**中国天然气产业发展面临挑战，但推动天然气产业协调稳定发展的基础条件**

和支撑因素未变，天然气产业持续稳步发展的总基调不变。同时，国际天然气供需总体宽松，天然气价格低位宽幅震荡，国内增储上产能力显著增强，供气安全保障能力进一步提升；体制机制改革继续深化，产业政策持续改进；疫情催生并推动的新产业、新模式、新业态的不断涌现，为天然气较快发展提供了有利空间。下半年要坚持目标导向和问题导向，保障各时段天然气供应高效、充足，确保"十三五"规划圆满收官。

综合预测结果显示，2020年全国天然气消费量约为3200亿立方米，比2019年增加约130亿立方米。预计全国天然气（含非常规气）新增探明地质储量约8000亿立方米；国产气量（含非常规气）为1890亿立方米（不包括煤制气），同比增长约9%，总体保持较快增长态势。进口天然气约1400亿立方米，与2019年基本持平或略有增长，预计进口管道气500亿立方米，进口LNG约900亿立方米。

立足国内资源，继续积极稳步推进天然气勘探开发，切实提高天然气稳定供应能力。重点做大四川、新疆、鄂尔多斯、海域四大油气上产基地，推动常规天然气产量稳步增加，非常规天然气较快发展。打造四川盆地"双富集气"生产基地，四川盆地是常规天然气和非常规天然气富集区，通过加大碳酸盐岩常规气和致密气、页岩气开发，推进产量继续增加。打造鄂尔多斯盆地"致密气"生产基地，通过加大致密气开发力度，推进多种资源综合勘探开发，提高资源开采水平。打造新疆地区"深层气"生产基地，加大塔里木盆地等山前深层超深层资源勘探开发，推进天然气增储上产。打造海域"深水气"生产基地，加快渤海天然气开发步伐，加强渤海、东海和南海北部深水区资源勘探开发，进一步加快增储上产步伐。加强统筹协调，分类处置、分级管控生态红线内天然气矿业权和勘探开发活动。

加快管网和储气设施建设，发力补齐天然气互联互通和重点地区输送能力短板，推动形成"全国一张网"。沿海 LNG 接收站扩建、新建工程持续推进，海外 LNG 资源进入国内通道进一步拓展；国家油气管网公司正式运行，"全国一张网"的管网布局加快形成，中俄东线管道中段及南段加快推进，青宁输气管道有望投产，天然气资源南北调配能力稳步增强；多措并举增加储气能力，压实上游供气企业和国家油气管网公司储气责任，加快储气库基地及储气设施重点项目建设。健全项目用海、用地、环评等协调机制，积极创造条件推动项目建设。

科学编制"十四五"规划，持续推进体制机制改革，推动天然气行业高质量发展。准确研判国际国内发展形势，突出以人民为中心的发展思想，突出以改革创新破解发展难题，着眼长远、统筹兼顾，科学编制《天然气发展"十四五"规划》，并按照规划加快重大管网等项目建设，确保管道运输能力满足经济社会发展需要。进一步推进油气管网公平设施开放进程，促进管道设施利用效率。继续坚定不移深化油气体制改革，尽快推动天然气矿业权改革和国家油气管网运营机制改革落地见成效，为建成运行高效的天然气市场体系打好基础。

结 束 语

世界新冠疫情和政治经济形势仍然严峻复杂，但中国天然气持续稳定发展的基本面没有改变，支持天然气高质量发展的要素条件仍在增加。

站在"两个一百年"奋斗目标的历史交汇点，中国将始终坚持"逐步将天然气培育成为中国主体能源之一"的战略目标，抓好党中央对天然气产业的各项决策部署和"六稳""六保"等政策落实。确保完成天然气"十三五"规划确立的主要目标，扎实推进"十四五"规划编制工作，科学制定天然气发展目标和路径，构建安全稳定、协调发展的天然气综合保障体系。

《中国天然气发展报告》白皮书已连续发布五年，期待《中国天然气发展报告（2020）》的发布进一步激发社会各界为天然气未来发展出谋划策的积极性。

诚挚感谢各相关部门、研究机构、行业学会、企业、国际机构及众多专家的大力支持和帮助。

感谢以下人员（按姓氏笔画排序）对《中国天然气发展报告（2020）》提出修改建议，以及在成稿过程中作出的贡献：

王连生　王国力　王晓庆　田　瑛　史云清　孙　智
孙　慧　孙耀唯　朱学谦　许睿谦　刘祥鹏　张玉清
李　伟　李　雷　杨　雷　杨驿昉　沈　鑫　陈进殿
陈珊珊　金之钧　金淑萍　周淑慧　姜向强　高安荣
唐永祥　唐金荣　曾兴球　蔡勋育

China Natural Gas Development Report
(2020)

Oil and Gas Department, National Energy Administration

Institute for Resources and Environmental Policies, Development Research Center of the State Council

Center for Oil and Gas Resource Strategies, Ministry of Natural Resources

Petroleum Industry Press

China Natural Gas Development Report (2020) Editorial Board

(in the order of surname by number of strokes)

Chairpersons:

    LIU Baohua   LING Yueming   LONG Guoqiang

Deputy Chairpersons:

    LIU Hong   GAO Shiji   XIE Chengxiang

Committee Members:

    WANG Jing   YE Guobiao   LI Zheng   LI Yinghua

    LI Jifeng   ZHANG Yinghong   WU Wenlai

    ZHENG Herong   ZHOU Peng   GUO Jiaofeng

    HAN Jingkuan   PAN Jiping

Coordinator:

    GUO Jiaofeng

Principal Institutions:

    Oil and Gas Department, National Energy Administration

    Institute for Resources and Environmental Policies,

        Development Research Center of the State Council

    Center for Oil and Gas Resource Strategies,

        Ministry of Natural Resources

Supporting Institutions:

    China University of Petroleum (Huadong)

    Research Institute of Standards Norms, Ministry of Housing and

Urban-Rural Development

China Petroleum Planning and Engineering Institute

Sinopec Petroleum Exploration and Production Research Institute

CNOOC Gas & Power Group Ltd.

Shanghai Petroleum & Natural Gas Exchange

Publication and Translation:

Petroleum Industry Press

Preface

Nowadays, the patterns of the global supply and demand for natural gas are subject to significant adjustments. The supply of natural gas resources is further eased, market competition is intensified, international trade methods become more flexible, and prices continue to drop. Since the beginning of 2020, the novel coronavirus (hereinafter referred to as "coronavirus") has spread, the world economy has declined, the volume of international natural gas trade has shrunk, and prices have fluctuated significantly. Presently, ensuring supply security and stabilizing market consumptions have become the new focuses of the global natural gas development.

2019 marks the 70th anniversary of the founding of the People's Republic of China, as well as the 5th anniversary of the implementation of the new energy security strategy: "Four Revolutions, One Cooperation". All departments, localities, and enterprises have consciously implemented the decisions and deployments of the Party Central Committee and the State Council. Remarkable achievements have been made by vigorously enhancing the explorations and developments of oil and gas, along with accelerating the construction of natural gas production, supply, storage, and marketing systems. 2019 was the year when the investment in exploration and development was highest during the "13th Five-Year Plan", and 2019 was also the year when reserves of natural gas along with its production had increased substantially. The establishment of China Oil & Gas Pipeline Network Corporation marks a critical milestone of the reform of the oil and gas system by "managing the middle and letting go of the two ends". Facing the impact of the coronavirus, all parties, taking the initiative, have made every possible effort to ensure a stable and consistent supply of natural gas, providing strong support for the prevention and control of the epidemic and stable economic and social developments.

Centering on the strategy of the "Six Stability" and "Six Protection", the next steps to be taken are (1) to focus on the construction of production, supply, storage, and marketing system of natural gas, (2) to keep vigorously strengthening the exploration of natural gas, (3) to speed up the reform of pipeline networks, (4) to make up for the shortcomings of gas storage capacities, and (5) to continue promoting high-quality development of natural gas industry.

CONTENTS

1. Stable Development of Global Natural Gas Industries in 2019 ... 1

   (1) Development Status of Natural Gas in the World 2

   (2) Development Status of Natural Gas in China 6

2. Acceleration of Reform Processes in China's Natural Gas Market in 2019 11

   (1) Upstream Natural Gas Market Reform 11

   (2) Midstream Natural Gas Market Reform 14

   (3) Downstream Natural Gas Market Reform 15

3. China's Natural Gas Industry Rises against the Trend in 2020 24

   (1) Review of Economic, Social, and Natural Gas Industry Developments in the First Half of 2020 24

   (2) Overview of China's Natural Gas Development in the Second Half of 2020 28

Concluding Remarks 33

1. Stable Development of Global Natural Gas Industries in 2019[1]

In 2019, the global supply and demand of natural gas continued to maintain an easing state, trade volumes grew rapidly, terms in long-term agreement contracts became more flexible, pricing methods became more diversified, and the proportion of liquified natural gas spot goods was further increased. China's natural gas production, supply, storage, and marketing system continued to improve. Remarkable achievements have been made by enhancing the exploration and development of natural gas. The construction of major infrastructures such as pipelines and gas storage facilities has been accelerated. The consumption scale of natural gas increases continuously. The consumption of natural gas is effectively guaranteed even during the winter peak periods.

---

[1] The reserves, production, consumption and trade volume data in this chapter are mainly from the *BP Statistical Review of World Energy (2020)*. Data on the trade contract pricing and oil prices of liquified natural gas is from IHS. The domestic natural gas reserves data are from the *National Oil and Gas Reserves Bulletin (2019)* of the Ministry of Natural Resources. The domestic natural gas production data comes from the National Bureau of Statistics and the National Development and Reform Commission. The natural gas import data are from the General Administration of Customs.

(1) Development Status of Natural Gas in the World

The production increased steadily, and the liquefaction capacity increased rapidly. The exploration of natural gas in the world has made a significant number of discoveries and the sea areas remain the global hotspots for natural gas discoveries. In 2019, the global discoveries on recoverable natural gas reserves were 2.1 trillion cubic meters with about 71.0% of them distributed in the sea. As of the end of 2019, the remaining global natural gas reserves were 198.8 trillion cubic meters and the reserve-production ratio was 49.8. In 2019, the global production of natural gas was 3.99 trillion cubic meters, the growth rate being 3.4% year-on-year, but the growth rate dropped by 1.6 percentage points. Amongst the global production of natural gas, gas production in North America was 1128 billion cubic meters with a growth of 7.4% year-on-year; natural gas production in the Middle East was 695.3 billion cubic meters with a growth of 2.1% year-on-year; natural gas production in Russia-Central Asia was 846.5 billion cubic meters with a growth of 1.9% year-on-year. The global natural gas liquefaction capacity reached 433 million tons per year with a growth of 9.5% year-on-year and the growth rate increasing by 1.7 percentage points. 10 liquified natural gas export terminal projects were added and a total of 11 production lines were put into operation, providing an additional capacity of 37.81 million tons per year with a growth of 21.4% year-on-year. The growth of global natural gas liquefaction capacity was mainly contributed by the United States, Russia and Australia. Particularly, the United States provided 59.8% of the growth of global natural gas liquefaction capacity.

The growth rate of consumption has declined, and the growth rate of North America and the Asia-Pacific region has slowed down. In 2019, the global natural gas consumption, accounting for 24.2% of the primary energy consumption, was 3.93 trillion cubic meters with a growth of 2.0% year-on-year, and the growth rate dropped by 3.3 percentage points. In North America, the natural gas consumption was 1057.6 billion cubic meters with an increase of 3.1% year-on-year. In the United States, the consumption of natural gas was 846.6 billion cubic meters with an increase of 3.3% year-on-year, but the growth rate dropped by 7.5 percentage points. The dropping of the growth rate was owed to warm winters slowing down the growth of heating gas demands. In the Asia-Pacific region, the consumption of natural gas was 869.9 billion cubic meters with a growth of 4.7% year-on-year. In Japan, the consumption of natural gas was 108.1 billion cubic meters with a decrease of 6.6% year-on-year. The nuclear power plant in Japan was reput into operations, reducing the consumption of natural gas. In Europe, the consumption of natural gas was 554.1 billion cubic meters with a growth of 1.1% year-on-year. In Europe, the price of coal increased by almost 70% and the price of natural gas went down, making the power generation using natural gas more economic. Hence, the demand for natural gas increased significantly in Europe.

The trade volume has continued to grow, and the liquified natural gas trade volume has rapidly increased. In 2019, the global trade volume of natural gas was 1.29 trillion cubic meters with an increase of 4.1% year-on-year and the trade volume accounted for 32.7% of the global natural gas consumption with an increase of 0.6 percentage points. Among the global trade volume of natural gas, the volume of pipeline gas trade was 801.5 billion cubic meters with a decrease of 0.5% year-on-year; the volume of liquified natural gas trade was 485.1 billion cubic meters with a growth of 12.7% year-on-year. The global trade of liquified natural gas spot goods accounted for 33.5% of the total liquified natural gas trade in 2019. The top five countries of liquified natural gas export were Qatar (107.1 billion cubic meters), Australia (104.7 billion cubic meters), the United States (47.5 billion cubic meters), Russia (39.4 billion cubic meters), and Malaysia (35.1 billion cubic meters). In 2019, the total increase of liquified natural gas exports was 54.5 billion cubic meters, with the United States (increase by 18.9 billion cubic meters), Russia (increase by 14.4 billion cubic meters), and Australia (increase by 12.9 billion cubic meters) ranking as the top three countries for liquified natural gas export. The top three countries of liquified natural gas import were Japan (105.5 billion cubic meters), China (84.8 billion cubic meters), and South Korea (55.6 billion cubic meters). The top three countries of a dramatic increase of liquified natural gas import were China (11.3 billion cubic meters), the United Kingdom (10.9 billion cubic meters), and France (10.1 billion cubic meters).

The prices of natural gas remained low, and contract forms have become more flexible. In 2019, due to the loose supply and demand of natural gas, prices of natural gas decreased globally. In the United States, the annual-average price of natural gas was 2.53 USD per million British thermal unit at the Henry Hub and the decrease is 19.0% year-on-year. In the United Kingdom, the annual-average price was 4.45 USD per million British thermal unit at the National Balancing Point and the decrease is 44.3% year-on-year. In Northeast Asia, the annual-average price of the Long-term Association was 9.43 USD per million British thermal unit and the decrease is 1.0% year-on-year; the annual-average of liquified natural gas spot prices was 5.95 USD per million British thermal unit and the decrease is 39.1% year-on-year. Among the contracts executed in 2019, 18.5% of the contract volume was supplied by suppliers in the resource pool mode, and nearly 90.0% of the recent contracts in the globe had no restriction on destinations.

(2) Development Status of Natural Gas in China

The exploration and development of natural gas in China were enhanced significantly, and the growth of both reserves and production made historical records. In 2019, 334.8 billion RMB was invested nationally on the exploration and development of oil and gas and the increase is 25.5% year-on-year. Out of the 334.8 billion RMB, 82.1 billion RMB was invested in the exploration, made a historical record. With the exploration of conventional natural gas, a series of significant discoveries have been made to add many new large-scale reserves areas: such as the discoveries in the Sichuan Basin, Ordos Basin, Tarim Basin, and other sea areas. Several breakthroughs have been made on shale gas in Changning-Weiyuan, Taiyang, and other blocks in the Sichuan Basin. Moreover, with the exploration of natural gas, discoveries of atmospheric shale gas have been made in the Nanchuan area. 1.58 trillion cubic meters of natural gas was discovered in the geological reserves in China, an increase of about 600 billion cubic meters year-on-year, made a historical record. Amongst the 1.58 trillion cubic meters of natural gas, 809.1 billion cubic meters of natural gas came from the newly discovered geological reserve of conventional natural gas, and 352.1 billion cubic meters of natural gas came from the new reserves which are technically recoverable. 764.4 billion cubic meters of shale gas was added with the discoveries of geological reserves, and 183.8 billion cubic meters of shale gas came from the new reserves which were technically recoverable. The national production of natural gas (including unconventional natural gas) was 177.3 billion cubic meters with an increase of 17.0 billion cubic meters year-on-year, setting a historical record. Out of 177.3 billion cubic meters of natural gas, 152.7 billion cubic meters was conventional gas production, 15.4 billion cubic meters was shale gas production, 5.5 billion cubic meters was coalbed methane production, and 3.68 billion cubic meters was coal gas production.

Imports have grown steadily, and import sources and subjects have become more diversified. In 2019, China imported 96.56 million tons of natural gas[1] (equivalent to

---

[1] Annual national import volumes and prices are based on the data from the General Administration of Customs; import data by country and enterprises are obtained from the statistical database of IHS.

135.2 billion cubic meters) with an increase of 6.9% year-on-year. In terms of the forms of import, 37.6% (36.31 million tons, equivalent to 50.8 billion cubic meters❶) of natural gas was imported through pipelines and 62.4% of natural gas (60.25 million tons) was imported as liquified natural gas. The sources of liquified natural gas import become much more diversified with Australia being the largest source (29.1 million tons), followed by Qatar (8.63 million tons), and then Malaysia (7.37 million tons). The proportion of liquified natural gas spot stock continued to increase. 21.3 million tons of spot liquified natural gas was imported, accounting for 35.4% of total liquified natural gas imports. The market entities, importing natural gas, increased in numbers. In addition to major oil and gas enterprises, locally state-owned, private, and Hong Kong-funded enterprises imported 4.41 million tons of liquified natural gas, accounting for 7.3% of China's total liquified natural gas imports.

The layout of the natural gas infrastructure has been further improved and the interconnections continue to advance. By the end of 2019, China had built more than 87000 kilometers of mainline gas transmission pipes, with a primary gas transmission ability of more than 350 billion cubic meters

---

❶ The conversation factor is 1 ton=1400 cubic meters.

per year. The completion and commission of the northern section of the Eastern Route of China and Russia manifested that oil and natural gas can be achieved through four major import channels (the northeast channel, northwest channel, southwest channel, and offshore channel). The multi-channel and multi-gas supply patterns in northern areas continued to improve, and the emergency gas supply ability was further enhanced. The Guangzhou Station of the Second West-East Gas Pipeline has completed the pressurization. Three compressor stations on the fourth line of Shaanxi-Beijing were put into operation. The first phase of the E'an-Cang pipeline was put into production. As of the end of 2019, 27 underground gas storage reservoirs had been built nationwide and the effective working ability reached 10.2 billion cubic meters, which represent a year-on-year increase of more than 3 billion cubic meters.

The consumption scale of natural gas continued to expand, but the growth rate slowed down. In 2019, the apparent consumption of natural gas was 306.4 billion cubic meters, which represents an increase of 8.6% year-on-year. The consumption of natural gas accounted for 8.1% of the primary energy consumption structure, with an increase of 0.3 percentage points year-on-year. From the perspective of the structure of consumption, urban gas and industrial gas remained the main sources of natural gas consumption, accounting for 37.2% and 35.0% of the total national consumption, respectively. The growth rate of gas consumption in chemical industries has rebounded and the growth rate of gas consumption for power generation has declined in stages. In perspectives of the regions of consumption, East China (annual consumption of 89.7 billion cubic meters, accounting for 29.2% of the national annual consumption) consumed most natural gas, followed by North China (59.8 billion cubic meters), Northwest China (39.6 billion cubic meters), and Southeast China (37.5 billion cubic meters). In perspectives of the consumption rates by provinces, 13 provinces consumed more than 10 billion cubic meters of natural gas. In particular, Jiangsu consumed more than 30 billion cubic meters, and two provinces (Guangdong and Sichuan) both consumed more than 20 billion cubic meters.

2. Acceleration of Reform Processes in China's Natural Gas Market in 2019

Since 2019, China has continued to promote the market-oriented reform of natural gas. In the upstream, market access has been released, the competitive transfer of mining rights has been comprehensively promoted, and the vitality of exploration and development has been stimulated. In the midstream, the fair opening of infrastructure to third parties was promoted by establishing a national oil and gas pipeline network company and by separating the transportation and marketing. In the downstream, the use of natural gas was expanded by deepening the reform of natural gas pricing and reducing the tax and fees.

(1) Upstream Natural Gas Market Reform

The reforms of the upstream oil and gas market have been deepened and the exploration and development of the oil and gas market were orderly liberalized. To implement the reform of the oil and gas system which was proposed by the Party Central Committee and the State Council and to vigorously improve the efforts of oil and gas exploration and development, the policies were issued successively: *Guiding*

Opinions on Promoting the Reform of the Property Rights System of Natural Resources Assets in a Comprehensive Manner, Special Administrative Measures for Foreign Investment Access (Negative List) (2019), and *Opinions on Promoting the Reform of the Management of Ministry Resources (Trial)*. These schemes opened the oil and gas exploration and exploitation market, introduced social funds through multiple channels to carry out oil and gas exploration and development, implemented stricter block withdrawals, urged enterprises to increase their exploration and development effort, integrated the oil and gas exploration and production system to ensure at the institutional level that enterprises can exploit the reserve right after the discoveries, adjusted the 2-year renewal of prospecting rights to a 5-year renewal to reduce the cost of enterprises and delegated the registration and transfer of coalbed methane mining rights to provincial natural resource authorities so as to mobilize local enthusiasm. As of July 30, 2019, restrictions on foreign investment in oil and gas exploration and development and other fields were eased and restrictions on limiting the exploration and development of oil and gas to joint companies and cooperation were removed gradually. This upstream segment continued to promote the Xinjiang pilot project, to push forward with the construction of shale gas pilot testing zones in north Guizhou and south Sichuan, to establish a comprehensive demonstration area for the exploration and development of shale gas in western Hubei, to encourage the pilot reform in the South China Sea, and to launch a comprehensive energy revolution reform pilot project in Shanxi.

Improve the subsidy policy for unconventional natural gas and encourage enterprises to accelerate the exploitation of unconventional natural gas. The *Supplementary Notice on the "Temporary Measures on the Management of Special Funds for Renewable Energy Development"* clearly stated that establishing special funds for the development of renewable energy to support the exploitation and utilization of unconventional natural gas such as coalbed methane (coal methane), shale gas and tight gas. The entities that exceed the output of the previous year were offered a cascade bonus depending on the degree of excess. The entities that fail to reach the output of the previous year, a deduction was applied according to the degree of shortages. For the increase of unconventional natural gas produced during the heating season, the excess coefficient conversion is offered for the bonus, according to the principle "More production in winter, more subsidies in winter".

(2) Midstream Natural Gas Market Reform

Establish a national oil and gas pipeline network company and promote the construction of a "nationwide network". By conscientiously implementing the spirit of the *Opinions on Deepening the Reform of the Oil and Natural Gas System*, the *Implementation Opinions on the Reform of Oil and Gas Pipeline Network Operating Mechanism*, and other documents, an oil and gas pipeline network company was established with state-owned capital holdings and diversified investment entities. The reform of systems and their mechanisms was deepened, promulgating *Measures for the Fair Opening of Oil and Gas Pipeline Network Facilities*, the realization of the interconnection and fairness of infrastructures was accelerated, and a fair and open information platform for oil and gas pipeline network facilities was being built, and ensuring open and transparent access to information and the environment of the market operation was optimized. With the establishment of China Oil & Gas Pipeline Network Corporation and the separation of transportation and marketing of other types of long-distance pipelines at various levels, it is conducive to the fair opening of midstream infrastructure such as pipeline networks, to third-party market entities. It is conducive to further accelerate the overall planning, construction and operation of the national oil and gas trunk pipeline network, promoting the interconnection of pipeline networks, and establishing a "national network". It is also conducive to further improve the efficiency of the transportation and allocation of hydrocarbon resources and to ensure a secure and stable supply of hydrocarbons.

Documents, such as *Implementation Opinions on Accelerating the Construction of the Capacity of Natural Gas Reserve*, were promulgated to further accelerate the construction of gas storage infrastructures and to enhance the reserve capacity of natural gas. The planning and construction layout of gas storage facilities were optimized, and areas with large peak-to-valley differences and rapid demand growths were guided to appropriately raise construction targets. The operation model of gas storage facilities was established and improved, the independent operation was promoted, and the investment recovery channels, such as pricing mechanisms was further improved. The policy supports, from perspectives of land, taxation, finance, investments and so on, were increased to encourage enterprises to make up the shortcomings in the construction of gas storage infrastructures, and to rapidly promote the improvement of gas storage capacities.

(3) Downstream Natural Gas Market Reform

Promote the use of natural gas for power generation and accelerate the development of natural gas for transportation purposes under local conditions and continue to play the positive role of natural gas in the prevention and control of air pollution. With the coordinated development in different regions, different resource endowments, and different methods of energy usage, the consumption of natural gas power general projects was steadily promoted. By the end of 2019, the installed capacity of natural gas power generation has exceeded 90 million kilowatts. Simultaneously, the *2020 Implementation Plan for the Global Sulfur Restriction Order on Marine Fuel* and other documents, have accelerated the promotion and application of low-sulfur fuel for ships. With the "Chinese version of the sulfur restriction order" that came into effect on January 1, 2020, liquified natural gas ships and liquified natural gas heavy-duty trucks are expected to continue to develop.

With effective implementation of tax and fee reductions, end-users earnestly enjoy the dividends of the reform. The *Notice on Adjusting the Prices of Natural Gas Base Stations* and other documents require that, based on the adjustment of the value-added tax rate (the natural gas tax rate is reduced to

9%), Considering the reduction of the value-added tax rate, the prices of benchmark gas stations shall be adjusted according in provinces, regions and cities to ensure that the dividend from the reduction of the lower value-added tax rate was returned to users. It is stipulated that the cost-profit margin of urban gas project installation expenses shall not exceed 10% in principle, thereby reducing the cost of gas for end-users, guiding the transformation and upgrading of urban gas enterprises in high-quality. In February 2020, a notice was issued to implement the off-season price policy in advance to reduce the gas cost of enterprises in stages within the framework of the current natural gas price mechanism, implemented the off-season price policy in advance to reduce the gas cost of enterprises in stages.

Special Column

Reform Policy for Upstream Natural Gas Marketization

Serial Number	Publication Date	Publisher(s)	Policy Name(s)
1	January 2019	Ministry of Science and Technology, Ministry of Finance	*Notice on Further Optimizing National Key R&D Projects and Fund Management* (No. 45 Document〔2019〕of the Ministry of Science and Technology and the Ministry of Finance)

Continue

Serial Number	Publication Date	Publisher(s)	Policy Name(s)
2	February 2019	State Council	*Decision on the Cancellation and Decentralization of a Batch of Administrative Licensing Matters* (No. 6 Document〔2019〕of the State Council)
3	April 2019	General Office of the Communist Party of China Central Committee, General Office of the State Council	*Guiding Opinions on Coordinating and Promoting the Reform of the Property Rights System for the Assets of Natural Resources*
4	June 2019	National Development and Reform Commission, Ministry of Commerce	*Special Administrative Measures for Foreign Investment Access (Negative List) (2019 Edition)* (Decree No. 25)
5	June 2019	National Development and Reform Commission, Ministry of Commerce	*Special Administrative Measures for the Entry of Foreign Investment in Pilot Free Trade Zones (Negative List) (2019 Edition)* (Decree No. 26)
6	June 2019	National Development and Reform Commission, Ministry of Commerce	*Catalogue of Industries Encouraging Foreign Investment (2019)* (Decree No. 27)

Continue

Serial Number	Publication Date	Publisher(s)	Policy Name(s)
7	June 2019	Ministry of Finance	*Supplementary Notice on the "Temporary Measures on the Management of Special Funds for Renewable Energy Development"* (No. 298 Document〔2019〕of the Ministry of Finance)
8	December 2019	Ministry of Natural Resources	*Opinions on Promoting the Reform of the Management of Mineral Resources (Trial)* (No. 7 Document〔2019〕of the Ministry of Natural Resources)
9	December 2019	National Energy Administration	*Measures for the Assessment and Evaluation of the First (Set) of Major Technical Equipment in the Energy Field (Trial)* (No. 89 Document〔2019〕of the National Energy Administration)
10	March 2020	Ministry of Finance, General Administration of Customs, State Administration of Taxation	*Notice on the Cancellation of the Management of Duty-Free Import Quotas for Offshore Petroleum (Natural Gas) Exploration Projects* (No. 5 Document〔2020〕of the Ministry of Finance, General Administration of Customs and State Administration of Taxation)

Continue

Serial Number	Publication Date	Publisher(s)	Policy Name(s)
11	March 2020	Ministry of Finance, General Administration of Customs, State Administration of Taxation	*Notice on the Cancellation of the Management of Duty-Free Import Quotas for Petroleum (Natural Gas) Exploration Projects in Specific Onshore Areas* (No. 6 Document〔2020〕of the Ministry of Finance, General Administration of Customs and State Administration of Taxation)

Natural Gas Midstream Market Reform Policy

Serial Number	Publication Date	Publisher(s)	Policy Name(s)
1	March 2019	Central Commission for Comprehensive Reform and Deepening of State Policy	*Implementation Opinions on the Reform of Oil and Gas Pipeline Network Operation Mechanism*
2	May 2019	National Development and Reform Commission, National Energy Administration, Ministry of Housing and Urban-Rural Development, General Administration of Market Supervision	*Measures for the Fair Opening of Oil and Gas Pipeline Network Facilities* (No. 916 Document〔2019〕of the National Development and Reform Commission and the National Energy Administration)

Continue

Serial Number	Publication Date	Publisher(s)	Policy Name(s)
3	October 2019	National Energy Administration	*Notice on Strengthening the Disclosure of Fair and Open Work-Related Information of Natural Gas Pipeline Network Facilities* (No. 76 Document〔2019〕of the National Energy Administration)
4	December 2019	National Development and Reform Commission	*Central Pricing Catalog* (Decree No. 29 Document of the National Development and Reform Commission)
5	April 2020	National Development and Reform Commission, Ministry of Finance, Ministry of Natural Resources, Ministry of Housing and Urban-Rural Development, National Energy Administration	*Implementation Opinions on Accelerating the Construction of the Capacity of Natural Gas Reserves* (No. 567 Document〔2020〕of the National Development and Reform Commission)
6	May 2020	Central Committee of the Communist Party of China, State Council	*Opinions on Accelerating the Improvement of the Socialist Market Economic System in the New Era*

Natural Gas Downstream Market Reform Policy

Serial Number	Publication Date	Publisher(s)	Policy Name(s)
1	March 2019	National Development and Reform Commission	*Notice on Adjusting the Price of Natural Gas Base Stations* (No. 562 Document〔2019〕of the National Development and Reform Commission)
2	June 2019	National Development and Reform Commission, Ministry of Housing and Urban-Rural Development, General Administration of Market Supervision	*Guiding Opinions on Regulating Installation Charges for Urban Gas Projects* (No. 1131 Document〔2019〕of the National Development and Reform Commission)
3	June 2019	National Development and Reform Commission, Ministry of Commerce	*Special Administrative Measures for Foreign Investment Access (Negative List) (2019 Edition)* (Decree No. 25 Document of the National Development and Reform Commission)
4	October 2019	National Maritime Administration	*2020 Implementation Plan for the Global Marine Fuel Sulphur Limit Order* (Announcement No. 20 Document of the Maritime Safety Administration Announcement)

Continue

Serial Number	Publication Date	Publisher(s)	Policy Name(s)
5	February 2020	National Development and Reform Commission	*Notice on the Phased Reduction of the Cost of Non-Residential Gas Consumption to Support Enterprises to Resume Work and Production* (No. 257 Document〔2020〕of the National Development and Reform Commission)

3. China's Natural Gas Industry Rises against the Trend in 2020

Since 2020, the outbreak of coronavirus has had a major impact on China's economic, societal and energy development. Consequently, the growth rate of the demand for natural gas has been suppressed significantly but still achieved a growth of 1.5% in the first half of year. 2020 is the closing year of the "13th Five-Year Plan" as well as the planning year of the "14th Five-Year Plan". The natural gas industry should continue to promote the high-quality development of the industry in accordance with the important deployment of the new energy security strategy of "Four Revolutions, One Cooperation".

(1) Review of Economic, Social, and Natural Gas Industry Developments in the First Half of 2020

Energy security has been tested during the coronavirus, and natural gas consumption in the first half of the year achieved a positive year-on-year growth. In the first quarter, China's economic growth was –6.8% and the added value of secondary and tertiary industries declined by 9.6% and 5.2%, respectively. The economic growth in the first half of the year was −1.6% and the added value of the secondary and tertiary industries fell by 1.9% and 1.6%, respectively. In the first half of 2020, due to the combined impact of the epidemic and the downward oil prices, the domestic oil and gas industry faced shocks and challenges. All departments, localities and enterprises have fully cooperated to win the battle against the epidemic in the oil and gas sector, and to resolutely protect the main battlefield against the epidemic and the national demand for oil and gas. The construction of natural gas production, supply, storage, and marketing systems is steadily progressing with scientific decision-making, and resuming major infrastructure projects such as the China-Russia Eastern Route and interconnection projects in a solid and orderly manner. Major projects such as the middle section of the Sino-Russian Eastern Route are proceeding in an orderly manner according to the established schedule. In the first half of 2020, natural gas consumption still maintained a positive growth rate with a year-on-year increase of about 1.5%. Factors driving the positive growth of natural gas consumption include declining domestic and foreign gas prices and increasing competitive natural gas prices. Urban gas consumption has been less affected by the epidemic and the heating season in some northern provinces and cities have been extended. Since the second quarter, the economic recovery has been obvious, and the resumption of work and production has led a steady rise in gas consumption for the industry and power generation.

In the first half of 2020, China's natural gas exploration efforts remained basically unchanged while production continued to grow strongly. Subject to new challenges and difficulties brought about by the coronavirus in the first half of 2020, investment in oil and gas exploration and development across the country have been generally stable, the amount of exploration work has steadily increased, and important discoveries have continued to be made in the Sichuan and Tarim basins. Natural gas production was 94 billion cubic meters, with year-on-year growth of 10.3%. Out of the overall production of natural gas, conventional gas production was 82.3 billion cubic meters, with year-on-year growth of about 8%, shale gas production was 9.1 billion cubic meters, with year-on-year growth of about 35%, and coalbed methane production was 2.6 billion cubic meters, with year-on-year growth of about 10%. China's natural gas production is expected to be 189 billion cubic meters (excluding the gas produced from coal) in 2020, with year-on-year growth of about 9%, maintaining a relatively rapid growth overall.

In the first half of 2020, structural differences in the

demand for natural gas were obvious. Firstly, the industrial consumption of natural gas gradually recovered from a negative growth rate to that of prior levels in 2019. Industrial gas consumption was subject to certain impacts during the early stages of the coronavirus outbreak. Then, the country implemented policies such as the phased reduction of non-resident gas prices in order to reduce the cost of gas for enterprises, achieving a gradual recovery of the industrial gas month by month. The cumulative gas consumption from January to June returned to the same levels as that of 2019 during the same period. Secondly, the urban consumption of natural gas maintained stable growth. In the first quarter, driven by the extension of the heating season in some northern provinces and cities, the urban consumption of natural gas maintained a steady growth. In the second quarter, the prevention and control levels were lowered successively, the floating population continued to increase, and shopping malls, restaurants, schools, et cetera. gradually resumed operations. The public service sector's demand for natural gas significantly improved and both together, promoted the first half of urban gas consumption to increase by more than 10% year-on-year. Thirdly, the consumption of natural gas for the power generation and the chemical industry was relatively significantly affected by the epidemic and declined in the first half of 2020.

(2) Overview of China's Natural Gas Development in the Second Half of 2020

In the second half of 2020, facing the impact of the coronavirus, the development of China's natural gas industry is facing challenges, however, the basic conditions and supporting factors that drive the coordinated and stable development of the natural gas industry have not changed. The overall tone of the natural gas industry's steady and continuous development remains unchanged. Simultaneously, the international supply and demand of natural gas are generally loose, natural gas prices are fluctuating widely at low levels, the domestic capacity to increase reserve discoveries and production has increased significantly, and the ability to ensure gas supply has been further enhanced. Institutional reforms continue to deepen, and industrial policies continue to improve. The emergence of new industries, new models and new business formats spawned and promoted by the epidemic, have provided favorable space for a faster development of natural gas. In the second half of the year, we must always adhere to the goal- and problem-oriented approach in order to ensure an efficient and adequate supply of natural gas, and to ensure a successful conclusion of the "13th Five-Year Plan".

The comprehensive forecast shows that the national natural gas consumption in 2020 will be about 320 billion cubic meters, an increase of about 13 billion cubic meters from 2019. It is estimated that the new proven geological reserves of natural gas (including unconventional gas) across the country will be about 800 billion cubic meters; domestic natural gas (including unconventional gas) will be 189 billion cubic meters (excluding coal gas), an increase of about 9% year-on-year and the overall rapid growth trend will be maintained. The amount of natural gas imported will be about 140 billion cubic meters which is basically unchanged compared to that of 2019 or slightly increased. It is estimated that 50 billion cubic meters of pipeline gas will be imported and about 90 billion cubic meters of liquified natural gas will be imported.

Based on domestic resources, the exploration and development of natural gas will be promoted actively and steadily, and effectively improving the capacity for stable supply of natural gas. Focuses should be put on the expansion of the four major oil and gas production bases in Sichuan, Xinjiang, Ordos, and the sea areas, promoting a steady increase in conventional natural gas production and rapid development of unconventional natural gas. The first is to build a "dual enrichment gas" production base in the Sichuan Basin which is an enrichment area for both conventional and unconventional natural gas. By increasing the development of conventional carbonate gas, tight gas, and shale gas, promoting the production to increase continuously. The second is to build a "tight gas" production base in the Ordos Basin. This will promote the comprehensive exploration and development of a variety of resources by increasing the intensity of tight gas development, and improving the level of resource extraction. The third is to build a "deep gas" production base in Xinjiang. The increase of natural gas reserves and production can be prompted by increasing the exploration and development of deep and ultra-deep layers resources in the piedmont areas such as the Tarim Basin. The fourth is to build a "deep-water gas" production base in the seas. The development of natural gas in Bohai Sea will be accelerated and the exploration and development of resources in the deep waters of the Bohai Sea, the East China Sea, and the northern South China Sea, will be strengthened to further accelerate the pace of increasing reserves and production. The overall coordination will be strengthened disposal classified, and hierarchical management and control of natural gas mining rights and exploration and development activities within the ecological red line.

Accelerate the construction of pipeline networks and gas storage facilities to make up for the shortcomings in natural gas interconnection and transmission capacity of key regions, and promote the formation of a "national network". The expansion and construction of coastal liquified natural gas receiving terminals will continue to advance, and channels for overseas liquified natural gas resources will be further expanded. China Oil & Gas Pipeline Network Corporation will officially be put into operation, and the formation of a "national network" pipeline network layout will be accelerated. The constructions of the middle and southern sections of the China-Russian East Pipeline will be accelerated. The Qingning gas transmission pipeline are expected to be put into operation, so that the north-south deployment of natural gas resources will be steadily enhanced. Multiple measures will be taken to increase the storage capacity of natural gas. The upstream gas supply companies and the national oil and gas pipeline network company will have full responsibility for gas storage. Moreover, the construction of key projects of gas storage bases and gas storage facilities will also be accelerated. The coordination mechanisms of the sea, land, and environmental assessment for projects will be improved and conditions will be actively created to promote the project constructions.

The "14ᵗʰ Five-Year Plan" will be scientifically formulated and both the reforms of institutional mechanisms and the high-quality development of the natural gas industry will continue to be promoted. Making an accurate assessment of the international and domestic development situation, highlighting people-centered development thinking, highlighting the use of reforms and innovations to solve development problems, focusing on the long-term development and considering the bigger picture are ways that will scientifically compile the "14ᵗʰ Five-Year Plan for Natural Gas Development". In accordance with the plan, the construction of major pipeline networks and other projects will be accelerated to ensure that the pipeline transportation capacity meets the needs of economic and social development. Further promoting equitable opening of oil and gas pipeline networks and improving the efficiency of their usage. Continuing to unswervingly deepen reform of the oil and gas system. This is to promote the reform of natural gas mining rights and the innovation of the national oil and gas pipeline network company's operating mechanism as soon as possible and achieve results so as to lay a solid foundation for the establishment of a functioning and efficient natural gas market system.

Concluding Remarks

The coronavirus outbreak and political and economic situations remain severe and complex, however, the fundamentals for the sustained and stable development of China's natural gas remain unchanged. The factors for supporting the high-quality development of natural gas are still surging.

Standing at the historical crossroad of the "Two Centenary Goal", China will always adhere to the strategic goal of "gradually cultivating natural gas into one of China's main energy sources", and vigorously implement the Party Central Committee's "Six Stability" and "Six Protection" policy, as well as all other decisions and deployments made for the natural gas industry.

China will Ensure the completion of the main goals that are established in the "13th Five-Year Plan" for natural gas, solidly advance the drafting of the "14th Five-Year Plan", formulate scientific goals and paths for natural gas development, and building a comprehensive security system for the safe, stable, and coordinated development of natural gas.

The *China Natural Gas Development Report* white paper

has been published annually for five consecutive years. It is expected that the publication of the *China Natural Gas Development Report (2020)* will further inspire all sectors of the community to significantly contribute ideas and thoughts to the future development of natural gas.

We would like to express our gratitude for the support and assistance provided by all the relevant departments, research institutions, industry associations, enterprises, international organizations, and participating experts.

Thanks to the following people (in the order of surname by number of strokes) for their suggestions to the revision of the *China Gas Development Report (2020)* and their contributions during the drafting process:

WANG Liansheng	WANG Guoli	WANG Xiaoqing
TIAN Ying	SHI Yunqing	SUN Zhi
SUN Hui	SUN Yaowei	ZHU Xueqian
XU Ruiqian	LIU Xiangpeng	ZHANG Yuqing
LI Wei	LI Lei	YANG Lei
YANG Yifang	SHEN Xin	CHEN Jindian
CHEN Shanshan	JIN Zhijun	JIN Shuping
ZHOU Shuhui	JIANG Xiangqiang	GAO Anrong
TANG Yongxiang	TANG Jinrong	ZENG Xingqiu
CAI Xunyu		